THE LITTL…
AL…
T…PS

WILLIAM FORTT

THE LITTLE BOOK OF ALLOTMENT TIPS

WILLIAM FORTT

A.
Absolute Press

Absolute Press
An imprint of Bloomsbury Publishing Plc

50 Bedford Square
London WC1B 3DP
UK

1385 Broadway
New York NY 10018
USA

www.bloomsbury.com
Absolute Press and the A. logo are trademarks of Bloomsbury Publishing Plc

First published in 2012.
Reprinted 2014, 2015.

A catalogue record for this book is available from the British Library.
Library of Congress Cataloguing-in-Publication data has been applied for.
ISBN 13: 9781906650759

Printed and bound in Spain by Tallers Gràfics Soler

‘I want death to find me planting
my cabbages’

Michel de Montaigne (1533–1592),
French philosopher and essayist

1

A good allotment is worth waiting for, so be patient.

Hold out for the allotment which is best and most convenient for you, rather than being in a rush to grab the first plot which becomes available.

2

How do you find an allotment?

First of all, contact your local council and ask them. If they have nothing available, try the National Society of Allotment and Leisure Gardeners (www.nsalg.org.uk/) or the Federation of City Farms and Community Gardens (www.farmgarden.org.uk/).

3

Ask around the neighbourhood.

If all else fails, try inquiring locally.

Many people have spare plots of land

they might be prepared to rent out to an enthusiastic gardener (even a beginner). So talk to neighbours, workmates, local farmers and friends. You never know what might come up.

4

Find an allotment **as near your home as possible.** The shorter the journey the better – especially important if you have to tend plants every day (think of watering in dry summers). You'll enjoy your gardening all the more if getting there is not too bothersome.

5

Get a transport system worked out. A car or at least a bicycle may be essential. Remember, everything for the plot will have to be carried there. This includes tools, seeds and watering cans as well as bulky items like compost and hoses. Then, of course, you'll have to **carry the produce back home.**

6

Remember: gardening can take up a lot of your spare time. So, if your leisure is limited,

think about sharing a plot with someone else.

Either cultivate half the ground each, or divide the work equally on the whole thing. Choose someone you can trust to do their fair share of labour.

7

Take a good hard look at the allotment site **before you sign up.** Is there a convenient water supply? Is your plot likely to be a frost pocket in winter? In which direction is it facing? Will it be shaded by trees or hedges in summer? Is the ground liable to get waterlogged or flooded?

8

The most important question is:

what's the soil like?

Get a rough idea by picking up a fistful and squashing it into a ball. If it sticks firmly together, it's clay. If it falls apart, it's sandy. These need improving with composts and other materials. If you're lucky, you'll have a nice dark loamy soil – not too sticky, not too dry.

9

Get to know your fellow allotment holders. They'll usually be happy to answer many of the queries mentioned in Tips #7 and #8 – and a lot more. The older hands will know about local problems (such as the likelihood of vandalism). Most gardeners are glad to dispense wisdom, advice and the odd seedling.

10

You may inherit **an overgrown plot,** full of brambles and other perennial horrors. if it's a large area, **clear the soil little by little,** a manageable patch at a time – but do the job thoroughly. Once a patch is weed-free and bare, you can start sowing or planting it.

11

Good tools will last a lifetime, so **buy the best you can afford.** The absolute essentials are: a fork and a spade; a rake, a hoe and a line with stakes at each end to mark out rows. A watering can and a good pair of gardening gloves will help, too. And if you're growing fruit you'll need secateurs.

12

If your plot has a shed,

is it safe to leave tools and other equipment there?

As before, get advice from other gardeners. If in doubt, take the tools home every time. Another option is to make the fork and spade handles removeable. Thieves are unlikely to pinch handle-less tools.

13

Make yourself comfortable.

At the very least, this means some kind of seat to rest on – a plank on upturned buckets will do.

Better still, put up **a cheap and simple shelter or shed** to keep off showers or cold winds while you drink your tea.

14

For rough digging of untended ground, use a spade rather than a fork. Turn over a clod, then chop it to bits with the spade edge. Also use the spade to slice off the turfy top section and bury this upside down at the bottom of the trench, where it will be covered with the next lot of soil and slowly rot down.

15

The obvious way to **get rid of weeds** is by **digging or pulling them out.** This is tough work, for you must be sure to extract all the roots of perennial weeds like couchgrass or bindweed, otherwise they'll appear again. But it's also effective and costs nothing – apart from sore knees or an aching back.

16

The best weed suppressor is a

layer of **mulch.** This **smothers and kills almost everything.** It can be organic (compost, animal manure, or cardboard covered with a layer of soil), which breaks down into the soil, or inorganic (black plastic sheet or even old carpet), which doesn't.

17

Divide the plot into **a series of deep beds.**

These are deeply dug (obviously), and no more than 1.2m (4ft) wide. This means you can reach the centre from either side and

never have to tread on the dug soil.

As a result, the soil never gets compacted, and remains easy to weed and fork through.

18

Lay narrow paths between the beds. This is what you'll walk or push barrows on (instead of squashing the dug soil). Hard paths are easier to maintain than grass. Use broken brick and stone, gravel or wood chips, and edge with whole bricks or slates to stop it spilling onto the soil.

19

Perennial weeds can be treated with a chemical herbicide.

Remember that this should only be done in the growing season, when there are leaves to aim at. Otherwise the spray may be ineffective. In general, use chemicals of this sort as sparingly as possible.

20

Be prepared to diversify. If this is your only piece of garden, you may want to produce **more than just vegetables.**

You could set aside an area for growing flowers, and another for soft fruit such as raspberries and blackcurrants. If you're planning a long stay, think about planting shrubs or even small fruit trees.

21

Harvest the rain. Drought is becoming more common, and you may be far from a tap. So **catch and store rainwater.** Buy a plastic water butt, or use anything handy, such as old oil drums or dustbins. If you have a shed, fix guttering and down pipes to direct the water to the tank.

22

Know your vegetable families.

They can be roughly split into **four main groups** – potatoes, roots (carrots, turnips etc), brassicas (cabbages, sprouts etc), and the rest (which includes onions, lettuce, beans and peas). Each group has different growing needs, frailties and strengths.

23

Know the rules and be considerate.

Most allotment societies have a code of conduct. This may cover anything from restrictions on what you can grow to weed control and rubbish disposal. Stick to the rules, and remember that thoughtless actions can ruin your neighbours' crops – and their tempers.

24

Rotation, rotation, rotation. If you grow one family of vegetables in the same place every year, specific diseases and pests will build up in the soil. So divide the plot into four sections and rotate what you grow in each – spuds one year, roots the next, onions and salads the next, and so on.

25

A compost heap is the heart of the garden.

Knock up a bin from pallets or scrap wood, then fill it with garden waste. This includes kitchen leftovers (no citrus or meat), grass mowings, non-perennial weeds, torn card and newspaper, plus a sprinkling of earth. Turn the whole thing once and leave for three months.

26

Keep improving your soil. Add as much humus (organic material) as you can, to help soil structure, and the ability to retain nutrients. Anything organic – composts, mulches, seaweed, grass mowings – will do a lot of good. Just spread them on top – earthworms will dig them in for you.

27

Growing plants need food, in the form of nutrients. Compost only provides a fraction of this. Make sure your soil has the correct balance of chemicals and trace elements. It can get these from materials such as blood, fish and bone meal, animal manure, volcanic rock dust or a commercial fertilizer.

28

When a bed is dug, **rake it thoroughly to get a fine and level tilth.** Get rid of stones, weed roots and other clutter. A well-raked surface makes it much easier to sow seeds evenly, and to pull out competing weeds later on. Good tilth also allows water to penetrate more evenly to the soil below.

29

Take the trouble to

sow seeds at the correct distance and depth.

Spacing (between both individual plants and rows) has a big effect on plant growth. Plant potatoes too closely, for example, and the crop will be smaller. Follow the instructions on the seed packet, or consult a trustworthy gardening book.

30

Make your own measuring stick

for marking out rows. Find a thin piece of timber 2 metres long. Using a tape measure, mark out metric measurements on one side (every 10 centimetres), with paint or a felt-tip pen. Then do the same for imperial measurements (in 3-inch units) on the other side.

31

You've measured your rows and scraped out furrows. **Before you sow the seeds, gently water the furrows.**

This gets moisture into the soil under the seeds, ready to create a nice humid atmosphere to start them germinating. Use a can with a fine rose so that you don't flood the furrow and compact it.

32

Sow seeds as thinly as possible. You don't want a tangled mat of shoots coming up, which needs major thinning out. This wastes seed and means you'll probably damage the remaining seedlings. Leave space between each seed. This is a fiddly job, but will give you stronger and healthier plants.

33

Rake the soil gently back over the seeds in the furrows.

Be careful not to disturb the seeds by being too forceful. Tamp down the soil – just as gently – with the head of the rake. Then give the bed another light watering.

34

Remember to mark the rows.

Sounds obvious, but it's easy to forget exactly what you've sown as the weeks go by. Write the crop's name on a stick, or slot the empty seed packet into a split piece of bamboo. To be doubly sure, keep a written record as well, with the date of sowing.

35

Start brassicas and other winter vegetables in a seed bed in a spare corner of the allotment. Here you can raise seedlings without taking up space in the main beds. By summer, early potato and bean crops will be gone, so you can transplant seedlings from the seed bed to take their place.

36

Be generous with water. Rather than just wetting the surface every day, give it a **good long soak** every three or four days. This means the moisture will soak right down to reach the roots of the plants, where it is really needed.

37

Raspberries are an ideal fruit to grow in an allotment. Not only do they crop heavily, they also make use of vertical space. Support them by tying to a series of wires stretched between two head-high posts. Summer-fruiting varieties have much the best flavour.

38

Currant bushes

take up a lot of space, but once established they will give you

wonderful crops year after year.

And they are a wonderful source of vitamin C. Plant black-, red- or whitecurrants 1.5 m (5ft) apart and learn how to prune them properly (it's too complex to explain here).

39

Everybody loves strawberries.

Unfortunately, so do snails, slugs and many other pests. When the fruit appears, cushion the straggling stems on **plenty of clean straw.**

This keeps the fruit dry, and discourages mould, mildew and molluscs.

40

Planning to be a long-term allotment holder?

Plant one or two fruit trees.

Apples, plums or pears on a dwarfing root stock will grow no higher than 4 metres (13 feet), and

bear fruit within three years. Alternatively, train them against a wall or wire supports.

41

A cage will stop birds ruining your fruit crop. If bushes, canes and low trees are grouped together, you can cover them with a single fruit cage. Sink posts at the corners, link with thick wire, and cover the whole with plastic netting. Remember to include an access point so that you can gather the ripe fruit.

42

Always have something growing. Use your allotment to its maximum capacity by **following one crop with another** from March through until late autumn. Even in October you can sow carrots and beans, and plant winter salad leaves. Garlic can go in as late as December.

43

Make your allotment child-friendly.

Kids usually love the glamorous jobs like picking strawberries or peas. Add to the fun with a paddling pool or a swing. Set them jolly tasks like making a scarecrow or painting plant labels. Give them their own section of garden, to grow whatever they like.

44

What's better than an allotment? Answer: two allotments!

As knowledge and passion grow, you may find one plot is no longer big enough for you. If there are spare plots available, why not take on another? Now you'll have room for more fruit, more flowers – maybe even a chicken run.

45

Get discounts on your seeds.

One massive advantage of belonging to an allotment association is that you can club together and make large seed orders. Many merchants offer as much as 50% discount on orders over a set value.

46

Mice love allotments – and so, unfortunately, do rats. Rodents cause damage and can spread disease, and must be controlled. The only effective solution is poison. Put the bait in secured lengths of drainpipe. Rats can't resist a tunnel, but most other animals will keep out.

47

How do you control slugs?

Pellets (the enviro-friendly kind) are effective killers, and so are shallow containers of beer. You can also keep the beasts out with a barrier of dry material such as sand or grit. It helps to keep ground clear of weeds or long grass where they can shelter.

48

An allotment looks like a free banquet to birds – especially big scavengers like pigeons, rooks and gulls. So protect the most tempting crops (tomatoes, raspberries, peas, young brassicas etc) with narrow-mesh netting over hoops of willow or thick wire.

49

Keep a weekly record of everything you do and grow. Compare your allotment and its produce year by year. This helps you to **spot your mistakes** and learn from them, and to **enjoy your successes.**

A journal is also the best place to work out your plans for the future.

50

An allotment is about more than growing food.

It's a place to get closer to the earth and nature. Bring wildlife to your plot – flowers and scented shrubs like buddleia attract insects, and berry or seed-bearing plants draw the birds. A pond is a magnet for frogs and many other wee creatures.

William Fortt

William Fortt is a gardener of long standing, whose cottage garden in Wiltshire, is famed for the beauty of its rare plants and the wonders of its many varieties of culinary and medicinal herbs. He has been an author for more than 30 years, with many books to his name.

THE LITTLE BOOK OF
BARBECUE
TIPS
ANDREW LANGLEY

THE LITTLE BOOK OF
BEER
TIPS
ANDREW LANGLEY
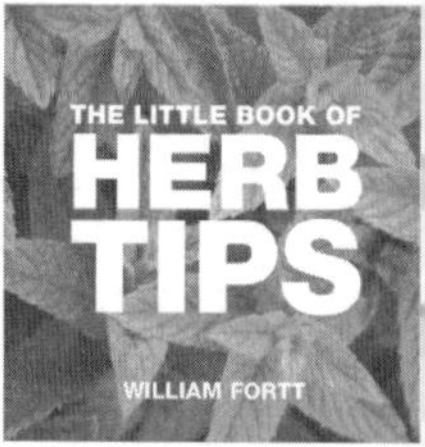
THE LITTLE BOOK OF
HERB
TIPS
WILLIAM FORTT

THE LITTLE BOOK OF
POKER
TIPS

THE LITTLE BOOK OF
GARDENING
TIPS
WILLIAM FORTT

THE LITTLE BOOK OF
CHEFS'
TIPS
RICHARD

THE LITTLE BOOK OF
SPICE
TIPS
ANDREW LANGLEY

THE LITTLE BOOK OF
GOLF
TIPS
PETER FRENCH

THE LITTLE BOOK OF
TIPS
SERIES

THE LITTLE BOOK OF
CHEESE
TIPS
ANDREW LANGLEY
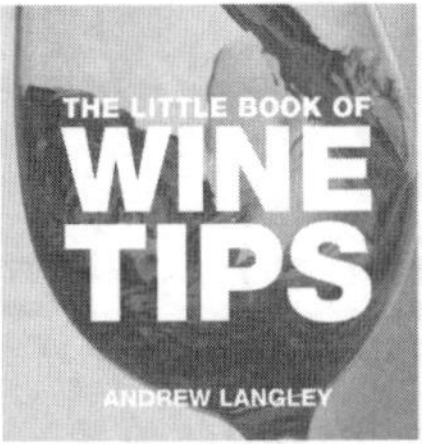
THE LITTLE BOOK OF
WINE
TIPS
ANDREW LANGLEY

THE LITTLE BOOK OF
AGA
TIPS 2
RICHARD MAGGS

THE LITTLE BOOK OF
COFFEE
TIPS
ANDREW LANGLEY

THE LITTLE BOOK OF
TEA
TIPS
ANDREW LANGLEY

THE LITTLE BOOK OF
AGA
TIPS 3
RICHARD MAGGS
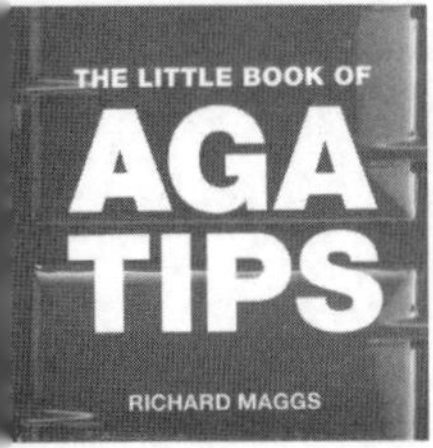
THE LITTLE BOOK OF
AGA
TIPS
RICHARD MAGGS

THE LITTLE BOOK OF
CHRISTMAS
AGA
TIPS
RICHARD MAGGS
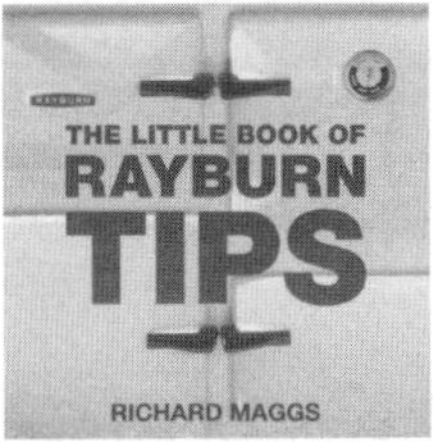
THE LITTLE BOOK OF
RAYBURN
TIPS
RICHARD MAGGS

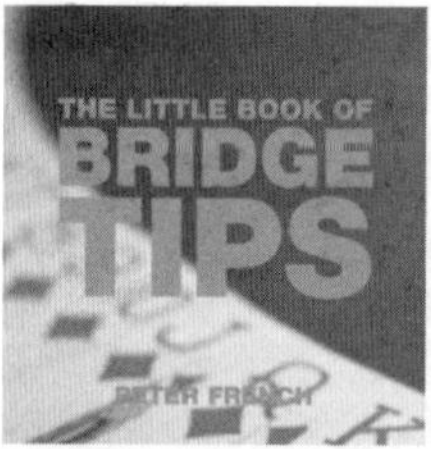
THE LITTLE BOOK OF
BRIDGE
TIPS
PETER FRENCH

THE LITTLE BOOK OF
CHESS
TIPS
PETER FRENCH

THE LITTLE BOOK OF
FISHING
TIPS
MICK DEVENISH

THE LITTLE BOOK OF
GREEN
TIPS
WILLIAM FORTT

THE LITTLE BOOK OF
KITTEN
TIPS
ANDREW LANGLEY

MARMITE
PAUL HARTLEY
THE LITTLE BOOK OF
MARMITE
TIPS

THE LITTLE BOOK OF
PUPPY
TIPS
ANDREW LANGLEY

THE LITTLE BOOK OF
WHISKY
TIPS
ANDREW LANGLEY

THE LITTLE BOOK OF
TRAVEL
TIPS
MEGAN DEVENISH

Little Books of Tips from Absolute Press

Aga Tips
Aga Tips 2
Aga Tips 3
Allotment Tips
Backgammon Tips
Barbecue Tips
Beer Tips
Bread Tips
Bread Machine Tips
Bridge Tips
Cake Baking Tips
Cake Decorating Tips
Champagne Tips
Cheese Tips
Chefs' Tips
Chess Tips
Chocolate Tips
Christmas Aga Tips
Chutney and Pickle Tips
Cocktail Tips
Coffee Tips
Cupcake Tips
Curry Tips
Fishing Tips
Fly Fishing Tips
Frugal Tips
Gardening Tips
Golf Tips
Green Tips
Grow Your Own Tips
Herb Tips
Houseplant Tips
Ice Cream Tips
Jam Tips
Kitten Tips
Macaroon Tips
Marmite Tips
Olive Oil Tips
Pasta Tips
Poker Tips
Puppy Tips
Rayburn Tips
Slow Cooker Tips
Spice Tips
Tea Tips
Travel Tips
Whisky Tips
Wine Tips
Wok Tips
Vinegar Tips

Ayrlie's garden
Auckland